Sky, Wind, and Stars

Sky, Wind, and Stars

by
Yoon Dong-joo

Translated by
Kyung-nyun Kim Richards
and
Steffen F. Richards

ASIAN HUMANITIES PRESS
(An Imprint of Jain Publishing Company)
Fremont, California

ASIAN HUMANITIES PRESS

Asian Humanities Press offers to the specialist and the general reader alike the best in new translations of major works and significant original contributions to enhance our understanding of Asian literature, religions, cultures and thought.

ASIAN HUMANITIES PRESS
[An imprint of Jain Publishing Company]
Web Site – www.jainpub.com

Acknowledgement is made to Korea Literature Translation Institute (LTI Korea) for financial assistance in the production of this book.

Library of Congress Cataloging-in-Publication Data

Yun, Tong-ju, 1917-1945.
  [Hanæul kwa param kwa pyæol kwa si. English]
  Sky, wind, and stars / translated by Kyung-nyun Kim Richards and Steffen F. Richards.
     p. cm.
  ISBN 0-89581-826-4
  1. Yun, Tong-ju, 1917-1945–Translations into English.
I. Richards, Kyungnyun K. II. Richards, Steffen F. III. Title.

PL991.96.T6H313 2003
895.7'13–dc21

                                                            2003010440

In memory of my brother,
Kang-nyun,
who so loved Korea.

Contents

Acknowledgment

I wish to express my deep gratitude to Mrs. Cha Hyung-soon (nee Heo), who so generously shared her memories of life in Yong-jung, Manchuria. Her memories of Yoon Dong-joo provided me with invaluable information in understanding the landscape of many of his early poems. My sincere thanks are also due to Professor Kwon Young-min of Seoul National University for his encouragement and support.

Grateful acknowledgment is also due to the Korean Literature Translation Institute (formerly Foundation) for its grant support for 1998-1999, without which this work could not have been possible. I wish for the continued growth and success of the Institute.

Kyung-nyun Kim Richards

Yoon Dong-joo

Yoon Dong-joo was born in Myong-dong Chon, a village in northern Manchuria on December 30, 1917, to a Korean family known for its strong patriotism and progressive thoughts. The paternal side of the family had moved to northern Manchuria in his great-grandfather's generation, and one of his uncles on his maternal side was a revered educator who established a school for the children of Korean residents in Manchuria. It was in this school that young Yoon Dong-joo began his primary education. The school taught him Korean and history, among other subjects, and he was exposed to an intense sense of identity as a Korean and of patriotism for his country.

His interest and talent for writing became manifest early in his youth. As early as age twelve, he started publishing his rhymes and poems for children in a mimeographed magazine called "New Myong-dong"[1] with the help of his childhood friend and cousin, Song Mong-kyu.[2] Most of his children's poems were written during this time.

After his primary education, he entered high school in Yong-jung, Manchuria, north of Myung-dong Chon. The school was called Eun-jin Middle School and was run by Canadian missionaries. His earliest dated poems ("A Single Candle," "Life and Death," and "No Tomorrow"), which bear the date of December 24, 1934, were written during this time. His practice of dating his poems seems to have begun at this time also.

For some unknown reason, he transferred to the famous Presbyterian school, Soong-sil High School, in Pyong-yang, in his senior year. However, after a semester, the school had difficulty with the Japanese authorities for resisting the order to pray at the altar of the Japanese Emperor, and Yoon left the school in protest. He returned to Yong-jung, but enrolled in Kwang-myung High School instead of returning to his old school. Throughout this period, he continued to write and publish his poems in school and church publications.

His father had hoped that Yoon would study medicine. When it was time for him to decide on a college education, Yoon, however, wanting to study literature, entered Yon-hee College (now Yonsei University) in Seoul, after much discussion with his grandfather and uncle. This was in the spring of 1938 when he was 21 years old. At Yon-hee, he studied languages and literature under such eminent scholars as Choi Hyun-bae and Lee Yang-ha. These scholars not only instructed Yoon and other young students in the subjects of their academic discipline, but they also imparted a strong sense of their own identity through extensive studies of Korean language, literature, and history.

Yoon was an avid reader and had an extensive library of some 800 volumes by the time he was a senior at Yon-hee. He read poets such as Chong Ji-yong, Kim Young-nang, Lee Sang, and Seo Chong-joo, and was especially fond of the works of Kierkegaard, Dostoyevsky, Valery, Gide, Baudelaire, Jammes, Rilke, and Cocteau.

An important aspect of his days at Yon-hee College was his experience of living in various boarding houses in Seoul. His close friend and cousin, Song Mong-kyu, had been under the suspicion of working for the resistance movement, and Yoon also was under surveillance, as he was closely associated with Korean intellectuals who were engaged in the resistance. He had to move from boarding house to boarding house in order to elude harrassment by the Japanese police.

In 1941, as a commemorative gesture for his graduation from college, Yoon compiled a collection of 19 poems with the title "Sky, Wind, Stars, and Poems." He intended to publish 77 copies and to distribute them to his friends and relatives. But the project was postponed when his trusted professor, Lee Yang-ha, advised him to wait for a more opportune time, as some of his poems might not pass the censorship of the Japanese authorities. Yoon Dong-joo then made three copies by hand: one for Professor Lee Yang-ha; one for his closest friend and roommate, Chong Byong-wook, whose copy survives; and one for himself. These poems were never published in his lifetime.

After graduation from college, Yoon returned to Manchuria and spent the summer there. Although he was an intellectual with a college degree and was considered an upper-class citizen, he volunteered to teach children in church schools and to help with chores on the family farm. He enjoyed reading and loved collecting books written in Korean as he thought the Japanese would eventually wipe out the use of Korean altogether. His demeanor was always neat and he was a man of modest manners.

In March 1942, he went to Japan and enrolled in Rikkyo University in Tokyo to study English Literature. At the same time, his cousin, Song Mong-kyu, enrolled in the Western History Department of Kyoto University. That summer, he returned to Manchuria for vacation but went back to Japan and transferred to Doshisha University in Kyoto.

In 1943, all students who did not volunteer for student military service were drafted. Just as Yoon was waiting to leave Japan for the summer, he was arrested on July 14, 1943. His cousin, Song Mong-kyu, who was attending Kyoto University, was also arrested at the same time. They were charged with "participation in the resistance movement" and were jailed in Kyoto. All of the manuscripts written during his stay in Japan were confiscated by the police, and he was forced to translate much of it into Japanese. He was indicted and convicted as part of the "independence movement" on March 31, 1944, and was serving a two-year sentence when he died on February 16, 1945, in a prison in Fukuoka. It was just six months prior to the establishment of Korea's independence from Japan, in August, 1945. The circumstances of his death suggest that it derived from chemical experimentation that had been conducted on prisoners. His cousin, Song Mong-kyu, who was a fellow inmate, also died in prison within a month of Yoon's death.[3]

Yoon lived his entire life under Japanese colonial rule. The places of his birth and death illustrate the degree of dislocation he experienced during his short lifetime: born the eldest son of an exiled family in desolate Manchuria, he died a prisoner of conscience in his oppressor's country. In spite of the social and political conditions he confronted every day, or perhaps because of them, he wrote poems of the utmost beauty and power. His poetic genius was endowed with a profound sense of truthfulness and sincerity. His poems are like gems that have been tested by fire.

Constructed of direct and simple language, his poems are free of rich symbolism and metaphor. But they are deep in meaning and evoke images of tranquility, tenderness, and soulful solitude. The body of work left by Yoon Dong-joo is not large: it consists of 97 poems, including the poems written for children, and four essays. However, his poems are considered some of the best of all time among contemporary Korean readers and he is one of the most studied poets in Korea today.

Yoon's poems speak of love and compassion. Love for "all things that are dying" (Foreword) and therefore love for all things that are living, compassion for "the children (who) do not know whose land they are in" (The Sunny Spot), for the "beggar boys" going over a mountain pass, (Turgenyev's Hill), for the women vendors (The Marketplace), for "the white-clad people" with thin waists (A Sorry Person). His compassion extends even to his own self (Self-Portrait).

In some of his poems, he is introspective and examines his own conscience and inner being. One aspect of this is his "shame" (Confessions), a shame experienced by an intellectual who is helpless at the loss of his nation's sovereignty to an alien power. A slightly different kind of shame appears in connection with the concept of original sin (Another Morning at the Beginning). Critics often argue that the source of his shame was in his inability to actively engage in rescuing his country from its bondage. Perhaps another way to understand the meaning of the word "shamefulness" may be through "humility," in some deeper religious sense.

By the time he was to graduate from college, he seemed to accept the condition he was in, however tentatively, and to "walk the road given to me" (Foreword). It is unclear, however, what this "road" was.

His last poem, written while he was in Japan, is "The Poem that Came Easily" (also translated as "The Poem Easily Written"), which speaks of Japan as a foreign country. In a time when Koreans were required to pledge their allegiance to the Emperor of Japan as his loyal subjects, the expression of alienation and independent identity from the imperial authority provided sufficient excuse for the Japanese to accuse him of betrayal and subversion. No wonder, then, that he was under constant surveillance by the Japanese police who were becoming increasingly paranoid as Japan became engaged in the Pacific War.

Yet his poems sing of hope and longing—longing for his lost self and nation, longing for his mother and homeland, longing for freedom and the eternity that transcend the conditions under which he had to live. The title of his intended poetry collection, "The Sky, Wind, Stars, and Poems", demonstrates how deeply he longed for space and freedom (sky), how affected he was by the forces of life (like the wind), and how his lofty dreams and high hopes shone like stars in the dark sky. And he juxtaposed his poems among such vast, free, and eternal elements. And he hoped for the day when he could "be happy and hold hands again (with friends) on some other morning" (Street Flowing).

Sadly, Yoon Dong-joo never saw the morning when he would be happy again nor his own poems published as a collection, let alone enjoy the popularity and admiration his poems now receive. But he did foresee that:

> . . . when winter has passed and spring comes even to my star,
> like the grass growing green over the graves,
> on the hill where my name is buried,
> grass will grow tall and thick with pride.

> —One Night I Count the Stars   (November 5, 1941)

More than half a century after his death, Yoon Dong-joo's poems find ever more resonance in the hearts of his fellow Koreans, who honor him with affection and pride. Kim Dong-gill best summarized the readers' feelings when he said, "The deep love expressed by the poet, Yoon Dong-joo, toward his people is directly tied to the spirit of resistance, and that is why it is so profoundly moving."[4]

Much of the exquisite beauty of Yoon Dong-joo's language has necessarily been lost in the translation to English, which is the language of a separate culture. Each of these languages has its own uniqueness, as do the cultures. Korean is a language endowed with so much expressive power and with such a unique sense of rhythm, that no other language could hope to capture them. However, I hope that the effort of our translation to convey something of this power and expressiveness has not been without some success, and that the reader might gain some inkling of these, and perhaps—is it too much to hope?—be led on to the study of Korean itself and into the beauty which lies there, hidden in the folds of its literary robe. Whatever the case, the gems of Yoon Dong-joo's poetry deserve to be shared with a wider world. It was with this in mind that I embarked upon this work of translation, and that I present his poetry now to the English-speaking reader.

Kyung-nyun Kim Richards
June 2000

Notes

1. Myung-dong is the name of the town in Manchuria where Yoon Dong-joo was born. It is also the name of the primary and middle school that his uncle established for the education of Korean children in Manchuria. It was a school known to promote patriotism, the preservation of Korean national identity through education in Korean history, and the ardent desire for independence from Japanese rule.

2. When Yoon Dong-joo's father and uncle went to Fukuoka to claim his body, they visited Song Mong-kyu. Song was quoted as saying that he has been receiving injections daily as a part of a special research project under the auspices of the University of Kyushu. He complained of the loss of weight and appetite as well as of extreme fatigue.

3. Omura Matsuo. "Report on the historical material relating to Yoon Dong-joo." *Yoon Dong-joo Yeon-koo (Studies on Yoon Dong-joo)*, pp. 513-530. Seoul: Mun-hak Sa-sang Sa, 1995.

4. Kim Dong-gill. "Si-in-eui Sarang (Love of the Poet)." *Hyun-dai Soo-pil Jip (Modern Korean Essays)*. 1973.

Foreword

Wishing not to have
so much as a speck of shame
toward heaven until the day I die,
I suffered, even when the wind stirred the leaves.
With my heart singing to the stars,
I shall love all things that are dying.
And I must walk the road
that has been given to me.

Tonight, again, the stars are
brushed by the wind.

November 20, 1941

A Single Candle

I smell the fragrance
of a single candle permeating my room.

Before the altar of light collapsed,
I saw the immaculate sacrifice.

The body, like the rib of a goat;
even the wick,* his very life—
the candle burns them all,
shedding tears and blood of pure white jade.

Even so, the candlelight dances fairylike,
enchanting, upon my desk.

Like a pheasant fleeing a falcon,
the darkness has escaped through my window,
and I savor the magnificent fragrance of the sacrifice,
which fills my room.

December 24, 1934

---

* "Wick," written in Chinese characters, literally means "heart and will."

Life and Death

Life sang the prelude to death again today.
When will this song end?

People of the world
dance
to the song of life which melts their bones.
They do not have the time
to think
about the terror at the end of the song,
before the setting of the sun.

Who was it that sang the song
as if etching an egg in the middle of the sky?

And who was it that ended this song
as if a rain shower had passed?

The dead,
whose bones are all that remain—
the victorious heroes over death.

December 24, 1934

On the Street

A street in the moonlight,
swept by the gusting wind;
a street in the northland.*
Under the pearls of the city,
the electric lights,
I swim like a small mermaid.
Two or three shadows of my body,
cast by moonlight and lamplight,
wax and wane.

On this street of anguish,
gray in the night,
where my heart is walking,
a whirlwind arises.
Lonesome though I am,
shadows in my heart
rise, one after the other:
blue dreams,†
rising and falling.

January 18, 1935

---

* i.e., Manchuria. Tr.
† i.e., of attending an institution of higher education. Tr.

Blue Sky

On that summer day
the passionate poplars
shook, arms outstretched,
and strove to caress
the blue breast of the sky,
in that narrow slip of shade under a boiling sun.

Beneath a sky reminiscent of a tent,
dancing clouds led
noisy showers
and thunder,
and escaped to the south.
The lofty blue sky, splayed
over the branches,
called forth full moon and geese.

A swelling young heart burns with ideals,
and on a day of autumn, a day of longing,
it scoffs at tears, at the falling leaves.

October 20, 1935

The Southern Sky

Swallows have two wings
on a gloomy autumn day.

One evening, when a frost has settled,
a young soul, longing for his mother's embrace,
intently roams the southern sky
on a single wing of nostalgia.

October 1935

A Clamshell

Shimmering, shimmering clamshell.
My sister found a clamshell
on the beach.

Here in the north,
a clamshell is a precious gift;
a clamshell is a toy.

Tumbling, tumbling, we're having fun.
The other half is lost
and the clamshell misses its mate.

Shimmering, shimmering clamshell.
It yearns, as I do, for
the sound of water, for the sound of the sea.

December 1935

Chicks

"Pew! Pew! Pew!
Mommy, we are hungry!"
So the chicks cry out.

"Cluck! Cluck! Cluck!
O.K. O.K. Hold on a second!"
So says Mother hen.

After a bit
the chicks
all went into
Mother's embrace.

January 6, 1936

The Bed-Wetter's Map

The map outlined on the cotton mattress
    hung out over the clothesline,
my younger brother drew last night
    when he wet his bed.

Is it a map of the Land of the Stars where Mommy is,
    which he visited in his dreams?
Is it a map of Manchuria where Daddy went,
    which he did to make money?

Early 1936

The Roof-Tile Couple

The roof-tile couple, on a rainy evening,
must miss their only son, who is lost.
Caressing each other, their backs bent,
they cry mournfully as their tears drip.

The roof-tile couple on the palace roof
must be longing for lovely, bygone days.
Caressing each other's wrinkled faces,
they stare up at the sky without a word.

ca. Early 1936

Doves

Seven little mountain doves, so adorable,
    I wish I could hold them in my arms.
On this clear Sunday morning,
    even the ends of the sky seem visible.
On the empty rice field, from which the rice has
    already been harvested,
they fight as they gather food,
    and exchange tales of hardship.

Stirring the calm air with two sets of slender wings,
    a pair fly away.
They must have remembered
    their babies at home.

February 10, 1936

Sunset

Through the crack under the sliding door,
sun rays draw, then erase,
the long line of the number "one."

A flock of crows fly over the roof:
two at a time, then three, then four.
They pass by again, and then again,
soaring, wriggling their bodies, in the northern sky.

And I?
I want to spread my wings in the northern sky.

March 25, 1936

Heart, 1

A silent drum
I try to beat
when I feel suffocated.

But, alas,
it is no better
than a mere sigh.
Whew! . . .

March 25, 1936

At the Summit

I reached the summit and saw below
roads like a go-board
and the river crawling like a baby snake.
The people must still be scattered about,
like black and white stones on the gameboard.

The noonday sun glares
only from the tin roofs.
The snail-paced train,
halted at the station, belches black smoke,
and totters forward again.

Wondering whether the tent of the sky
will plummet and cover the roads,
I yearn to climb to higher ground.

May 1936

On a Day Like This

On the day the five-color flag* and
    the flag of the rising sun† dance
atop the two friendly stone posts of the front gate,
the children across the border rejoice.

Sheer boredom descends on them
as they study the dry subjects of the day,
for they are still too simple to understand
what the word "contradiction" means.

On a day like this
I long to call on
my obstinate friend, whom I have lost.

June 10, 1936

---

* of Manchuria
† of Japan

The Sunny Spot

A spring breeze of the land, laden with yellow dust,
swirls away and beyond like a Manchurian windmill.

The shimmering rays of the April sun caress
every strand of their sorrowful hearts as they lean
        against the wall.

The two children playing "Redraw the Map,"*
do not know whose land they are in:
they lament the short reach of their fingers!

Stop, lest the shallow peace
be broken!

June 26, 1936

---

* A neologism of the poet. A kind of children's game of drawing maps
on the ground using the span between the thumb and middle finger. The
object of the game is to gain more territory.

Mountain Forest

When the ticking of the clock beats in my heart,
        (tic-tic, tic-tic),
I grow anxious and the forest on the mountain calls me.

The deep, dark forest, steeped in a thousand years
        of its ancient past,
must have the karma to embrace my single, tired body.

From above the black swaying of the forest,
darkness comes and crushes my young heart.

The evening wind shakes the leaves,
swooshing, making me shudder with fear.

Early summer frogs croak in the distance.
Remote are the past times when villages now lost existed.

Only the stars twinkling through the trees
lead me to hope for a new day.

June 26, 1936

The Chicken

Over the six-foot-square chicken coop
was blue sky,
but the chickens that had lost their land and freedom
railed against a life of toil
and cursed the bitter labor of production.

The foreign Leghorns
rushed out from the gloom of the chicken coop.
One clear afternoon in March,
a flock of birds also rushed out from the school.

The chickens were busy
scratching in the melting mulch
with their short legs
and feeding with hungry beaks:
until their eyes fumed a ripe red.

Spring 1936

Heart, 2

Deep is the winter night
as I move about, hugging the fire-crock,
from which the fire has long since gone out.

My heart, reduced to ashes,
trembles at the quivering of
the papered door.

July 24, 1936

A Dream Shattered

I awake from a dream,
out of a deep fog.

The singing skylark
has escaped and flown away.

It is not a meadow of golden grass
on which we sang our song of springtime.

The tower has crumbled,
the tower of my red heart. . . .

The tower, etched in marble with my fingernails. . . .
Not a chance during a storm at night!

Alas! The field has become desolate—
what tears and sobbing!

The dream has been shattered;
the tower has collapsed.

July 27, 1936

Laundry

Their two legs draped over the clothesline,
the white laundry whisper one to another in the afternoon.

The radiant July sun hangs quietly
just above the gentle laundry.

1936

A Broom

Cut away a little, this way and that,
and it comes out a jacket.
Cut it the long way, and it comes out a
gun.

> My big sister and I
> snipped away the paper with our scissors.
> Mother spanked my big sister and me once
> on our bottoms with a broomstick, saying
> the room was a mess!

> No, no! I know!
> That little broomstick hit us
> because it did not want to sweep
> the floor!

Mad at the mean ol' broom, I hid it in the closet.
Next day, Mother was in big trouble
looking for her broom.

September 9, 1936

Rain in the Sun

It comes down like a maiden,
softly, ever so softly—the rain in the sun!
Let's welcome it all together!
>   Let's hope the rain will grow five or six feet tall,
>   as tall as corn stalks.
>   The sun is smiling—
>   smiling at me!

There is a bridge across the sky,
a shimmering rainbow!
Let's sing out with joy!
>   Come on, friends!
>   Let's dance together!
>   The sun is smiling,
>   because it is happy.

September 9, 1936

The Chimney

From the low chimney of the hut in the mountain valley
rise puffs of smoke in the middle of the day: but why?

Some fellows must be roasting potatoes:
their dark twinkling eyes gathered around,
their mouths blackened with charcoal,
they tell a story with each potato.

From the low chimney of the hut in the mountain valley
rises the gentle smell of roasting potatoes.

Fall 1936

What Do They Live On?

People by the sea
eat the fish they catch.

People in the valleys of the mountains
eat the potatoes they roast.

People on the stars—
what do they live on?

October 1936

Spring, 1

Our baby sleeps soundly
in the warmest spot of the room,
snoring.

The cat purrs,
next to the stove.

A little breeze blows
gently through the branches.

The avuncular sun
sparkles in the middle of the sky.

October 1936

The Sparrows

The front yard, after autumn has passed,
is a sheet of white paper
on which sparrows practice their handwriting.

"Chirp, chirp," they repeat with their beaks:
with their feet, they practice their writing.

All day long they practice their writing,
but the only thing they can write is "chirp!"

December 1936

The Letter

Big Sister!
This winter again
the snowfall is heavy.

Shall I place in a white envelope
a handful of snow
and write no words
nor put on any stamps
and simply mail it to you
as neat as can be?

The land where you went,
they say, has no snow.

ca. December 1936

Stocking Patterns

Mother,
why are you saving the paper
Older Sister used to practice her calligraphy?

I did not know it,
but Mother put my stocking on the paper
to cut out a pattern
with her pair of scissors.

Mother,
why are you saving the pencil stubs
I threw away?

I did not know it,
but Mother put the pattern over the cloth
and, wetting the tip of the pencil in her mouth,
traced the pattern with dots
to make my stockings.

Early December 1936

The Snow

The snow has fallen
down, dazzling, so white
my eyes blink—
blink-blink-blink!

ca. December 1936

Morning

Swish, swish, swish.
The tail of the cow has chased the dark away
with a gentle whipping.
The pitch darkness had deepened before first light.

Now morning in this village is ample
as the rump of a cow fattened on grass.
The villagers, who lived on soybean porridge,
cultivated their crops all summer, shedding sweat.

On leaf after leaf, drops of sweat form, on every one of them.

I inhale deeply on this placid morning,
again and again.

1936

Winter

Under the eaves,
bundles of turnip greens
turn crispy
cold.

On the street,
balls of horse droppings
freeze,
drop by drop.

Winter 1936

The Sunset Turns into Ocean

Another day sinks . . . and sinks languidly
into the dark blue waves.

Wha. . . What is that school of fish flying across
the painted sea?

Seaweed like fallen leaves,
each so sad.

The bright painting of a landscape hangs
     in the western window;
the sorrow of an orphan biting the tie-string of his coat.

Having resolved to set out on my maiden voyage,
I lie around on the floor of my room . . . and lie around.

When the sunset turns into ocean,
today, again, so many boats will have submerged
among the waves with me.

January 1937

Tricked

Knock, knock, knock!
Please open the door!
Let me spend the night!
    Who could it be, out
    in the cold, in the deep of night?
I opened the door
and saw the tail of the black dog
that had fooled me!

Cluck, cluck! Cluck, cluck!
It laid an egg!
Little One, go get it quick!
    When the little one ran over to look,
    not an egg was found.
That rascally hen
hoodwinked me
in broad daylight!

1937

The Two of Them

The sea is blue
and so is the sky.

The sea is endless
and so is the sky.

I throw a rock into the sea
and spit at the sky.

The sea grins;
the sky is mum.

1937

Fireflies

Let's go! Let's go!
Let's go into the woods!
To gather pieces of the moon,
let's go into the woods!

     Fireflies, on the last night of the month,
     become pieces of the shattered moon.

Let's go! Let's go!
Let's go into the woods!
To gather pieces of the moon,
let's go into the woods!

1937

The Night

The donkey in the barn
let out a single bray: haw!

The baby woke with a start
at the braying: awng!

Light the lamp for me!

Father gave the donkey
a layer of hay.

Mother let her baby
suckle her breast.

The night returned to its sleep
and silence.

March 1937

The Marketplace

In the early morning, women gather in the marketplace,
carrying baskets brimming with the weariness of life—
on their heads, on their backs,
in their arms.
Women gather. . . .

Showing every detail of their poor lives,
they are pushed and pulled. . . .
All are shouting for their lives . . . and struggle.

All day long they measure their bundles of life
with tubs, scales, and yardsticks.
When darkness falls, the women depart,
carrying on their heads the bitterness of life they
      have exchanged.

Spring 1937

Moonlit Night

Pushing back the white waves of the flowing moonlight,
I walk over shadows cast by thin trees.
My footsteps toward Mt. Puk-mang* are heavy;
my heart, in the company of solitude, indeed sorrowful.

In the graveyard I imagine someone . . .
but no one is there.
Only the stillness is soaked in the white waves,
here and there.

April 15, 1937

---

* Mt. Puk-mang is a small mountain in the Province of Henan, China, where many aristocrats and famous personalities are buried. Thus it is known as a grave-site. Tr.

Landscape

The green ocean beneath the spring breeze
looks precarious, as if it would pour down at any moment.

The buoyant waves, like the fullness of a gathered skirt,
seem so delightful, as if they would fold together.

A red flag at the end of the mast
flutters like a woman's hair.

*   *   *   *

With this vivid view before and behind me,
I would like to walk for an entire day:

under a gloomy sky in May,
to the hill embroidered with colors of the sea, in panel
        after panel.

May 29, 1937

Thermometer

A thermometer hung by the neck against a cold marble post,
suddenly a column of mercury five-feet six-inches high, its
thin waist fated for inspection:
the heart is clearer than a glass tube.

An animal in popular opinion, neurotic, its veins simple,
it wastes its energy from time to time forcefully swallowing
the cold saliva that rises like a fountain.

Contrary to when the winter cold of Soo-dol's* room is
        below zero,
the campus in August seems ideal, sunflowers are in
        full bloom;
on a day that brings your blood to a boil. . . .

Yesterday it poured down rain, but today the weather is fine.
"Go out into the hills, into the woods in your shirtsleeves . . . ,"
I quietly whispered to myself.
I did so, without realizing it. . . .

Perhaps I must truly fall into line with the season of the
        century . . .
jumping off the fence when all I can see is the sky,
and keeping our place in history.

July 1, 1937

---

* A male first name. Tr.

The Downpour

Lightning, then the rumble of thunder:
a thunderbolt must have struck the city in the distance.

The sky an inkstone turned upside down,
the rain pours down like arrows.

In my garden, the size of the palm of my hand,
a lake has formed, as cloudy as my heart.

The wind turns like a toy top;
the trees cannot steady their crowns.

I invite reverence into my heart
to taste the sky of Noah's time.

August 9, 1937

Contemplation

The neat strands of my hair are the eaves of a tiny hut.
The ridge of my nose tickles me, as if disturbed by
    my whistling.

My eyes are loosely shut like a small, push-out window.
Tonight, love seeps in everywhere, like the dark.

August 20, 1937

The Sea

The wind the sea brings
sprays and cools.

Every branch of the pine tree is coy, and recoils,
its neck bent at an angle.

The sea pushes in,
and is pushed out.

Waves taller than the breakwater
soar up and seem a waterfall.

The children gather on the beach
to wash their hands in the brimming water.

The sea grows more sorrowful
under the singing of the sea gulls. . . .

How the sea today, in returning,
looks back again and again!

September 1937

Afternoon in a Mountain Valley

My song is more
a mournful echo.

The shadow cast
on the valley road
is all too sad.

My thoughts this afternoon?
Oh, how sleepy I am!

September 1937

*Pi-ro-bong**

Looking down at
Man-sang,*

my knees quiver
and clatter.

The white birch aged
during its youth.

A bird
becomes a butterfly.

A real cloud
turns to rain.

My clothes
are cold.

September 1937

---

* Pi-ro-bong is one of the highest peaks in the famed Keum-Gang
Mountain Range, from which one has a magnificent view of the "ten-
thousand" granite peaks known as Man-sang or Man-mul-sang (lit. the
shapes of ten-thousand things). They are so named because the unique
shapes of the peaks seem to show all the creatures of the earth. In 1998,
Mount Keum-Gang, which is located in North Korea, became accessible to
South Korean tourists through a special arrangement between a South
Korean travel agency and North Korean authorities. Tr.

At the Window

Every recess
I go to the window.

—Windows give living lessons.

Please build me a roaring fire.
Cold is settling into the room.

A single maple leaf seemed
to spiral:
perhaps from a small whirlwind.

Nevertheless, when the sun's rays shine brightly
on the cold windowpane,
I can tell the school bell is about to ring.

October 1937

His Last Words

In the room awash with light,
his last words were mere movements of his lips:

—My son, they say, went to sea to hunt for pearls;
   my first son, they say, fell in love with a woman diver:
   Look out to see if they are coming. . . .

The last breath of a father lonely during his lifetime:
Sorrow clouds his closing eyes.

A dog barks from a remote house;
cool blue moonlight flows over the ribs of the door.

October 24, 1937

The New Road

Across the stream and into the woods,
over the hill and on to the village
lies the road that I am traveling.

Yesterday, today:
my road, a new road.

Dandelions bloom: magpies fly by;
a young maiden passes.
The wind rises.

My road is always new:
today, tomorrow. . . .

Across the stream and into the woods,
over the hill and on to the village.

May 10, 1938

A Rainy Night

Crash! The sound of waves breaks against the ribs of the door
and scatters the dreams of my sweet slumber.

My sleep is disturbed as if by a school of black whales,
and I can think of nothing to calm myself down.

I turn on the light and carefully straighten my nightclothes.
Midnight.
A prayerful petition.

Afraid that Kangnam, the land I long for, will be
      flooded again,
I feel a solitude greater than I would longing for the sea.

June 11, 1938

Palace of Love

My dear Soon, when was it that you came into my palace?
And when was it that I entered yours?

Our palace
was a palace of love, where ancient customs reigned.

Dear Soon, like a doe, close your crystalline eyes.
I, like a lion, will groom my tangled mane.

Our love was only deaf-mute.

Before the hot flame of the sacred candle goes out,
run out the front door, Soon!

Before darkness and wind strike the window,
I will disappear through the back door
to a faraway place,
eternal love in my arms.

And now there is a quiet lake deep in the forest for you;
and for me, treacherous mountains.

June 19, 1938

The Miracle

Shall I thoroughly clean my feet
and try, ever so gently, walking
over the lake as though I were the dusk?

It is indeed a miracle
that I was called to come
to this lake:
yet no one called me.

Today somehow
I keep toying with
love, self-reprimand, jealousy:
as if they were gold medals.

But I promise I will wash these all away
among the waves on the water without a lingering thought:
I pray You call me out upon the lake!

June 19, 1938

An Impressionist Painting of My Younger Brother

On his red forehead, the moonlight was frosted cold:
my younger brother's face makes a sad painting.

Halting him,
I gently hold his young hand and ask,
"What will you be when you grow up?"
"A human being."
My brother's sad, truly sad answer.

Slowly letting go of his hand,
I look him in the face again.

The moonlight was soaked cold on his red forehead:
my younger brother's face makes a sad painting.

September 15, 1938

A Sorry Person

A white cloth is wrapped around her black hair
and white rubber shoes are caught on her rough feet.

Her white jacket and skirt hide her pathetic body
and a white band cinches her slender waist.

September 1938

Red Pepper Field

Among wilted leaves,
revealing its bright red flesh,
the red pepper grows ripe under the hot sun,
like a young woman coming of age.

Grandmother lingers about the field
holding her basket.
The child sucking his thumb
follows around the grandmother.

October 26, 1938

Sunlight and Wind

Having wet my finger with saliva,
I poked a hole, a second and a third,
in the paper of the door
to watch Mommy
go off to the market.
I poked a hole, a second and a third.

The sun shone bright in the morning.

Having wet my finger with saliva,
I poked a hole, a second and a third,
to see if Mommy was coming
back from the market.
I poked a hole, a second and a third.

The wind blew fair in the evening.

ca. 1938

Sunflower Face

My big sister has the face
    of a sunflower.
As soon as the sun rises,
    she goes to work.

The sunflower has the face
    of my big sister.
She comes home
    with her face down.

ca. 1938

Baby at Dawn

At our house
we don't even have a rooster.
When Baby
cries for Mother's milk,
only then is it dawn.

At our house
we don't even have a clock.
When Baby
whimpers for Mother's milk,
only then is it dawn.

ca. 1938

Cricket and I

Cricket and I
had a talk on the grass.

Crickitty crick,
crickitty crick.

We promised to let
no one else know,
no one else but the two of us.

Crickitty crick,
crickitty crick.

Cricket and I
had a talk in the night,
the moon up high, ever so bright.

ca. 1938

Echo

The magpie crowed
and an echo came back,
an echo that went
unheard.

The magpie heard
the echo though.
The echo he heard
by himself.

May 1938

Like the Moon

On a still night, when the moon waxes
like the rings of a growing tree,
love, alone like the moon,
grows like such aging rings,
filling my heart to aching.

September 1939

Turgenyev's Hill

I was on my way over the hill when three beggar boys
passed me by.
The first boy carried a basket on his back and
in it were cider bottles, cans, metal scrap, old socks,
and more: it was full of junk.
The second boy's was the same.
The third boy's was the same.
Their unkempt hair, their blackened faces,
their blood-shot eyes full of tears, their lips blue and
colorless, the tattered rags on their backs, and their torn
bare feet—
ah, what horrible poverty had engulfed these young boys!
My heart stirred with pity.
I searched my pockets: a thick wallet, a watch, a
handkerchief. . . .
I had everything one might need.
But I did not have the courage to simply hand these
things out.
I just kept running my fingers over them.
Thinking at least to talk to them, to be friendly,
I called out, "Hey, kids!"
The first boy turned merely to glance at me, his eyes red.
The second boy did the same.
The third boy did the same.
Then they went on over the hill chatting among
themselves,
having nothing more to do with me.
No one now was on the hill
and dusk was gathering.

September 1939

Water from the Depths of a Mountain Valley

A sufferer, a sufferer:
even among the waves of skirts,
water springs up deep in my heart,
but there is no one to talk with tonight.
I cannot join in singing with the clamor of the street.
I sit by the stream as though I have been singed,
and leave love and work to the street.
Quietly, ever so quietly,
I shall go down to the sea,
I shall go down to the sea.

ca. September 1939

Self-Portrait

Coming round the mountain, I go up alone to
the solitary well at the edge of the rice field
and peer in, quietly.

Inside the well, the moon is bright, the clouds flow by,
the sky spreads out, and a light blue wind blows;
autumn is there.

And a man is there.
I turn away because I hate the man, somehow.

Pondering over him as I set out to leave, I feel sorry for him
and go back and look in: he is still there.

Again I turn away hating the fellow.
I think of him, again setting out, and begin to miss him.

Inside the well, the moon is bright, the clouds flow by,
the sky spreads out, a light blue wind blows;
autumn is there, and a man, like a memory.

September 1939

A Youth

Here and there, autumn, like leaves that have turned, is sadly dripping. Spring stands ready at every spot from which the leaves have fallen, and the sky looms above the branches. If you look far up into the sky, your brows will turn blue. If you rub your warm cheeks between your hands, blue will come off on your palms. I look at my palms again. A clear river flows along the lines of my hand: a clear river is flowing, and in the water, I see a sorrowful face in love—the beautiful face of Sooni! I close my eyes in reverie. The clear river is still flowing, and still I see the sorrowful face in love—the beautiful face of Sooni!

1939

Eight Blessings
—Matthew 5:3–12

Blessed are they who mourn.
Blessed are they who mourn.
Blessed are they who mourn.
Blessed are they who mourn.
Blessed are they who mourn.
Blessed are they who mourn.
Blessed are they who mourn.
Blessed are they who mourn,

they shall grieve forever.

ca. December 1940

A Consolation

A mean spider had spun a web between the banister in the back garden of the hospital and the flower garden, where footsteps don't often reach. So the young man taking in fresh air could see it well from where he lay.

A butterfly flying among the flowers fell into the web. Struggling, the yellow wings only became more entangled. Like an arrow the spider moved in and wrapped up the butterfly, spinning its endless thread. The man sighed a long sigh.

The only consolation I could offer the man, who had lost his chances by falling ill and had suffered at his age more than his share of hardships, was to mess up the spider's web.

December 3, 1940

Hospital

Her face concealed in the shade of an apricot tree
as she lies in the garden behind the hospital, a young woman
is sunning herself, her legs white past her white
dress. Even after the best part of the day, no one,
not even a butterfly, comes to visit her, who is
said to be suffering from tuberculosis. Not even
the wind stirs among the branches of the apricot tree,
which knows nothing of sadness.

I am here for the first time, no longer able to endure
my mysterious affliction. But my elderly doctor does not
understand his young man's illness. He says I don't
have a disease. These excessive trials, this excessive fatigue:
I must hold my temper.

The woman gets up, tidies her dress, picks a
marigold from the flower bed and pins it to
her breast, and disappears into the ward. Hoping she
will quickly regain her health—and I mine—
I try lying down where she has just been lying.

December 1940

A Terrifying Hour

Who is it that's calling me?

In the shade of the large leaves still shooting up green,
I still have some breath remaining.

I, who have never once raised my hand;
I, who do not even have a piece of the sky
to which I can raise my hand and point:

Is there a place in the sky
to keep my only body,
that you should be calling me?

On the morning of the day I die,
after I have finished my work,
the leaves will fall without grieving. . . .

Please stop calling me!

February 7, 1941

Snowy Map

On the morning Sooni is due to leave, my silent heart is brimming over with words. Heavy snow is falling forlornly and covers the map which stretches far out into the distance outside the window. There is no one in the room when I look around. The walls and ceiling are white. Is it even snowing inside? Is it really true you have left, all alone, a history being lost? Words that I should have said before you left, are now written in a letter, but I don't know where you are going, or to what street or village, to be under whose roof. Is it true that you remain only in the depths of my heart? I cannot follow your small footsteps because the snow keeps covering them up. When the snow melts, flowers will bloom in each of them. And if I go out to look for your footprints among the flowers, snow will fall in my heart for the entire twelve months of the year.

March 12, 1941

Morning at the Beginning

On a morning neither in spring
nor in
summer, fall, or winter,

a red flower bloomed
in the blue sunlight.

The night before,
the night before,
everything was made ready:

Love lay with the serpent,
poison with the young flower.

1941

Another Morning at the Beginning

All is white with snow.
The telephone poles ring
and I hear the words of God.

What revelation can it be?

When spring comes
soon
I will commit sin and
my eyes
will open.

When Eve finishes her labor
of giving birth,

I will cover my shameful part
with a fig leaf,

and sweat will form on my brow.

May 31, 1939

Until the Dawn Comes

Will all who are dying
please dress in black.

Will all who are living
please dress in white.

And put them together,
tucked neatly, into one bed.

Whenever they cry,
give them Mother's milk.

And when dawn comes,
the trumpet will sound.

May 1941

The Cross

The sun was following me,
but it is now caught on the cross
on top of the church.

How can I get up
that high on the steeple?

No sound comes from the bell:
I might as well whistle and hang around.

If I were permitted my own cross,
like the man who suffered,
blessed Jesus Christ,

I would hang my head
and quietly bleed
blood that would blossom like a flower
under a darkening sky.

May 31, 1941

Go with Your Eyes Closed

Children who adore the sun!
Children who adore the stars!

The night is dark:
go with your eyes closed!

Go, scattering the seeds
you have!

Should you stumble over a stone,
open the eyes you have closed!

May 31, 1941

Sleepless Nights

One.
Two.
Three.
Four.
. . . .

Such nights indeed
are many.

Est. June 1941

The Night I Returned

As if returning from the world, I now return
to my narrow room and put out the light.
To keep the lamp lit is too tiresome a chore,
for it is an extension of the daylight. . . .

Now I need to open the window to air out
the room. As I calmly look outside, it is just as dark
as inside, and although the world looks exactly like
the one I know, the road I took
in the rain is still soaking wet.

Finding no way to purge myself of the rage of the day,
I slowly close my eyes:
sounds flow within my heart;
my thoughts are now ripening on their own,
like an apple.

June 1941

A Street Without Signs

When I stepped onto the platform of the train station,
no one was there to meet me.

All were strangers, or
looked like strangers.

The houses had no signs:
less worry about being discovered.

No signs in electric lights,
in red,
in blue.

At every corner
kindly gaslights were lit.

Were I to take them by the arm,
they would all be good people,
every one of them.

Spring, summer, autumn, winter—
they return according to their order.

1941

The Wind Is Blowing

Where does the wind come from,
and where does it go?

The wind is blowing,
and there is no reason why I suffer.

Is there no reason for my suffering?

Not one woman have I loved.
Nor have I ever mourned the times.

The wind keeps blowing
as I stand on the rock.

The river keeps flowing
as I stand on the cliff.

June 2, 1941

Yet Another Home

The night I returned home
my white bones followed me
and lay down in the same room.

The dark room gave out
on the universe
and the wind blew
like a voice from heaven.

Peering down at my white bones,
so finely worn away and
pulverized by the wind amid the darkness,
I wonder who it is whose tears are being shed.
Am I crying?
Is it my white bones?
Perhaps my beautiful soul?

A steadfast dog howls
in the darkness through the night.

The dog howling in the darkness
must be the one that is driving me away.

Let me go! Let me go!
Let me who am being driven away, let me go!
Let me go to yet another beautiful home,
stealing away from my white bones!

September 1941

The Road

I lost it.
Not knowing what I lost or where,
I go out to the street,
my hands in my pockets.

Stone after stone after stone, in endless array:
the road runs along a stone wall.

The wall, with its iron gate shut firmly,
casts a long shadow along the road.

The road led on, from morning to evening
and from evening to morning.

My tears falling as I gaze upon the stone wall,
I lift up my eyes:
the sky is shamefully blue.

I am walking this road without a blade of grass
because I remain on the other side of the wall,

and the reason I am living is
only because I am looking for what I have lost.

September 31, 1941

One Night I Count the Stars

The sky that the seasons pass through
is filled with autumn.

I feel as though I can count, without trouble,
all the stars in the depths of autumn.

The reason I cannot now count
all the stars being etched in the depths of my heart,
one and two at a time,
is that morning comes too soon;
night still remains until tomorrow,
and my youth is not yet spent.

For one star, a memory;
for one star, love;
for one star, loneliness;
for one star, longing;
for one star, a poem;
for one star, Mother. Mother.

Mother, I try calling each star something beautiful: the
names of the children I shared a desk with in primary school;
the names of the foreign girls, like Pae, Kyung, and Ok; the
names of the young women who are already mothers; the
names of our poor neighbors, and of the dove, puppy, rabbit,
mule, and deer; and the names of poets, like Francis Jammes
and Rainer Maria Rilke.

All of them are so far away,
like the stars that are infinitely distant.

And Mother,
you are in far northern Manchuria.

Longing for something,
I wrote my name
on the hill where so much starlight has fallen,
and then buried it.

Perhaps the insects drone through the night,
mourning over my shameful name.

But when winter has passed and spring comes even to my star,
to the hill where my name is buried,
the grass, like that growing green over graves,
will grow lush and proud.

November 5, 1941

My Liver

On a sunny rock by the seaside,
let me spread out my wet liver to dry.

Like the hare escaped from the depths of the Caucasus,*
let me circle round the liver and keep watch over it.

You, emaciated eagle that I long have kept!
Come and prey upon it without fear!

You must grow fat
and I must grow thin. But,

Dear Turtle!
I will never, never again, fall into the temptation of the
    Dragon Palace.

Prometheus! Pitiful Prometheus!
Because of his sin of stealing the fire,
he must sink forever, a millstone tied around his neck.
Prometheus!

November 29, 1941

---

* The hare (and the turtle mentioned below) appears in the "Legend of
the Hare," in which the turtle lures the hare to the undersea Dragon
Kingdom. The only cure for the ailing Dragon King requires the liver of
a hare. The hare, however, narrowly escapes death by using the ruse
that his "liver," the object of the Dragon King's desire, is so precious and
sought after that he has hidden it in the depths of the mountains. Believing
this, the turtle brings the hare back to land and the hare escapes to the
mountains ridiculing the turtle for his gullibility. Tr.

Confessions

There, in the patina-green bronze mirror,
I can still see my face.
What dynastic legacy is it
that makes me so ashamed?

Let me make my confession concise, in one line:
—What joy has sustained me
    for twenty-four years and one month?

Tomorrow, or the day after, on some joyous day,
I will have to write another line of confession.
—Why did I make such shameful confessions then,
    at such a tender age?

Night after night let me polish the mirror
with the palm of my hand and the sole of my foot.

Then, in the mirror, someone sad
will appear, walking away
alone, heading beneath a meteorite.

January 24, 1942

White Shadow

On the street corner, the dusk gathering,
you listen quietly, your ears tired after the day,
and you hear the footsteps of the dusk in motion.

Was I smart enough
to hear the footsteps?

Now that I have foolishly come to understand everything,
I am sending back so many of my selves—
suffered deep within my heart for so long—
to their own homes, one by one.
The white shadows disappear silently
into the darkness and around the corner.

White shadows:
the white shadows that I have loved with so much longing.

Having sent back all of my selves,
I turn around in the back alley, empty,
and return to my room soaked with the dusk.

May I graze contentedly on the grass all the day long,
like a dignified sheep, with deep conviction.

April 14, 1942

Street Flowing

Fog is flowing in the gloom. So also the street. But where are the wheels of this streetcar, and that auto, flowing? They have no harbor in which to moor. They carry so many wretched. The street is sunk in fog.

I stand next to a red mailbox on the street corner, in the midst of the flow. The faint street lamp does not go out. What does it symbolize?
My dear friend, Park! And Kim! Where are you now? The fog flows on without end.

"Let's be happy and hold hands again some other morning": I write a note and drop it into the mailbox, and stay up all night to wait. The postman will arrive, a giant, his golden buttons and golden badge making him glorious: a happy visitation of the morning.

Tonight, the fog flows on, without end.

May 12, 1942

Lovely Memory

One morning, as spring was approaching, I was waiting at
a little station in Seoul for a train, as if waiting for Hope
and for Love.

Barely casting a shadow on the platform,
I lit a cigarette.

My shadow exhaled a shadow of cigarette smoke.
A flock of pigeons flew by, unabashedly, one by one,
revealing as they did the undersides of their wings in the sun.

The train, having told me nothing new,
has taken me this far.

Now spring is gone. In a quiet room of a boarding house
        in a Tokyo suburb,
I still miss, as I would Hope and Love, being on that old street.

Today, again, the trains have passed by several times,
        meaninglessly.

Today, again, I shall linger upon the hillside near the station,
waiting for someone.

—Ah! Youth! Stay there a long time!

May 13, 1942

A Poem That Came Easily

The night rain whispers outside the window
of my six-mat room, in an alien country.

The poet has a sad vocation, I know:
should I write another line of poetry?

Having received my tuition from home in an envelope
soaked with the smell of sweat and love,

I tuck my college notebook under my arm
and go off to listen to the lecture of an old professor.

Looking back, I see that I have lost my childhood friends:
one and two at a time—all of them.

What was it that I was hoping for,
and why am I simply sinking to the bottom alone?

Life is meant to be difficult:
it is too bad
that a poem comes so easily to me.

My six-mat room in an alien country:
The night rain whispers outside the window.

I light the lamp to drive out the darkness a little,
and I, in my last moments, wait for the morning,
which will come like a new era.

Extending a small hand to myself,
I offer myself the very first handshake,
tears, and condolences.

June 3, 1942

Spring, 2

Spring was flowing in my veins like a brook,
babbling. On the hillside near downtown:
forsythia, azalea, and the bright yellow cabbage flower.

I grow like a tuft of grass,
having endured the long winter.

O happy skylarks!
Rise up joyfully from whatever field you happen to be in,

as the azure sky
is so dizzyingly high up. . . !

1942

The Canyon

The mountains ran in two lines.
The stream shouted, at frequent
bottlenecks.
The summer sun aboard the clouds
rushed to cross the valley.

Along the mountainside,
young boulders shot up as lumps here and there,
like the horns of a calf:
the soft hair of the dappled cow
has grown green along the mountain ridge.

A traveler in the valley,
returning home after three years,
was tramping the ground,
tamping it hard as he stepped
(with the bare legs of an egret . . .).

His old shoes were tied together and hung
on the end of his cane.
A few magpies flew by, their young at their heels.
The valley was silent—like the heart of our traveler.

Summer 1936

Grief

Following the solitary moon of our century,
I longed to walk to places I am familiar with,
and perhaps to those I am unfamiliar with.

As if to fly away in the dark of night,
I leap from my bed to walk out alone
into the endless wilderness.
Lonely shall this heart of mine be.

Ah! This young man is as sad
as a pyramid!

August 18, 1937

The Rose Fell Ill

The rose fell ill,
but there is no neighborhood
to move it to.

Should we send it up into the mountains
in a covered wagon all alone?

Should we send it out to sea,
to the mournful sound of a steamship horn?

Should we send it high up into the stratosphere
in an airplane, its propellers roaring?

Never mind all that.

Bury it instead in my heart
before my growing son
wakes from his dreams.

September 1939

No Tomorrow

  —A young heart kept asking:

Someone said, "Tomorrow, tomorrow":
well, "When is tomorrow?"

You sleep at night and dawn comes:
then it is "tomorrow."

When I woke from my sleep
and looked for the new day
it was not tomorrow—
it was today!

Listen up everyone! Listen, my friends!
There's no tomorrow!

December 24, 1934

Airplane

The propeller in front
turns faster than the
sails of a windmill.

Once aloft, high in the sky,
it is not as fast as when
it rose from the ground:
it seems out of breath.

An airplane
cannot flap its wings
like a bird,
and always
roars—
it must be out of breath!

Early October 1936

Pockets

The pockets were worried,
having nothing to fill them.

When winter came,
two fists filled them up
full.

1936

Dog

In the snow
the dog

frolics,
printing flowers.

1936

Home in My Hometown

—I called out from Manchuria

Why did I come here,
dragging my old straw shoes
across the River Tuman,*
to this desolate land?

My cozy hometown
down under the southern sky
where my mother is—
how I miss it!

January 6, 1936

---

* The River Tuman flows along the northeastern edge of North Korea,
providing a natural demarcation between Manchuria and the Korean
peninsula. Tr.